Sectio

Monster

Three in the morning, my eyes still open

Thinking bout the hearts I've broken

All the stupid things I've said

As well as those I've left unspoken

A tear drops from my hateful eye

Down my face, by and by

You say my heart has turned so black

It looks as though the midnight sky

Easy come, easy go

A simple life I'll never know

I owe it all to one so heartless

Colder than the frigid snow

Can you hear the shadows calling?

Whispers, moaning, screaming, bawling

They float amongst the dark ether

The nighttime realm through which I'm falling

This realm is where I shall remain

Until I cut her every vein

I, Aetheros, shall get revenge

My kiss of death be sure as rain

By Dakota Stanley

<u>Wrapped In Vines</u>

Everyday that passes by

Is one less worry in my heart

One less tear falls from my eye

That's one day further we're apart

One day closer to being free

Away from your hateful acid rain

One step closer to being me

A me that's happy, no more pain

One day I'm not getting beat

Distanced from your drunken wrath

I would think this very neat

One more night; do the math

Never once abused again

No more empty solitude

I'll find solace in a friend

No more monster parental feud

I'll find love, I'll have protection

One who heals me in my soul

She will show me her affection

Once together, I'll be whole

When that day finally shines

Beyond the sky my soul will soar

My heart forever wrapped in vines

Until my life is nevermore

By Dakota Stanley

The War

Walls so bare and empty

Carrying nothing but years of pain

The sound of a broken heartbeat

Explodes like bombs inside my brain

It seems as though my mind

Is as a cripple in his bed

The only difference being

This cripple's in my head

He lies there without a thought

Letting my heart lead the way

A broken heart with broken strength

Has broken every day

It seems the days are darker

As each one passes by

Sometimes I lie here wondering

If today's the day I die

A thought that's oddly welcomed

Embraced completely by my heart

A weary mind and broken heart

No longer forced apart

A time of peace draws near

The war is finally done

This day has gotten closure

To a beautiful setting sun

By Dakota Stanley

Broken Love

You cannot heal me

Can't be healed 'cause I'm broken

Broken by her love

By Dakota Stanley

Anger and Hatred

Anger and hatred

Things that destroy us inside

Are now my vices

By Dakota Stanley

Nocturnal Gift

The clouds in my life

Have given way to the moon

Giving me the night

By Dakota Stanley

Tragedy of a Broken Father

My son, my child, my heir

Why were you taken from me?

I see your smile in the mirror

But only in myself

Must he have been intoxicated?

Drunk on that specific night?

His selfishness took your life

How unfair

Why not take me?

You were but a child

An innocent child

MY innocent child

Dear spirits, tell my son I love him

Help him find peace

Make him see that I love him, truly

It's okay little one

You mustn't linger any longer

I will bring justice upon this drunken driver

I swear it

I swear it to you

My son, my child, my heir

By Dakota Stanley

Dark Ether

What is the dark ether, you ask?

It is found in the night

A realm of psychic quiet, serenity

A dimension where those of daylight sleep

Their minds, their souls, are utterly silent

Except those nocturnal beings which exist

Existing strongly in this darkness

Dark ether is that chill that blankets you

It blankets you only at night, when all is tranquil

It is the fear that seizes your breath, your life

This ether is darker than the darkest night

Making the darkest night sky seem aglow, afire

Ancient thoughtforms call to you

Will you answer?

It seems only respectful, polite

You are in their realm, their domain

A realm not meant for those to whom it does not beckon

A grave mistake this would be, to enter uninvited

For the ancient thoughtforms who lurk here

They shall be perturbed, enraged

Those whom they beckon, use wisely this gift

To be frivolous is not wise, nor useful

You are a guest

Take care

For this is the dark ether

By Dakota Stanley

These Walls

These walls will destroy you

They will crush your soul

Your very essence of being

They will crush it!

As sanity dissipates, you grow weak

Tired, tampered, they poison you

Your consciousness of what, "is," seeps

It seeps through the cracks in these walls

Do you hear them talking?

I do

They want to devour me

Devour you

Devour us

If only I could be free

Free from this madness that entombs me

Free to laugh, to love, and to live

O' but the time has come

The time has come to pay my dues

Pay them to the Keeper for it was he

He to which I was bound, was it not?

Yes!

Yes, it was!

I committed crimes against my fellow man

All was for not, 'twas worthless

Do not make the same mistakes I have

For these walls

These walls will destroy you

By Dakota Stanley

<u>Tool</u>

Darkness closes in

On this bleeding, lonely soul

My consciousness is fading

In fear, you are waiting

Wondering if you should just let go

But no, it can't be so

How could you lose me

At the height of our love?

Not knowing that I'm too far gone

Been this way for so damn long

You're too self-absorbed

To know that you're wrong

Such a fool, such a tool

Since the start I was broken

Just biding my time

Your love was my crime

My punishment is thus;

To wander the world, in pain

Insane was I to refrain

From the things that I craved

As I ranted and raved

Now I'm falling and falling

Into the abyss

That I have created

My rage will be sated

If only, if only

I could reanimate you

Bring you back from the dead

Or could they be true

That this is all in my head?

By Dakota Stanley

Section II: Decay

Heroin

A love so vivid, fire and ice

Burning up my frozen heart

Snakebite poison feels so nice

Blowing all my veins apart

Lift me up, let's fly away

Go to that place we know so well

We shall float around all day

Jump from heaven down to hell

It doesn't matter how you're dressed

Nor the color of your skin

Whatever you may think is best

Let's load you up and just begin

Again and again this cycle goes

Pain and pleasure shows the truth

Foes are friends and friends are foes

Eye for eye, tooth for tooth

Walls of pleasure dripping blood

From the things you've done to me

Lying facedown in the mud

One last breath is ecstasy

By Dakota Stanley

Looking Into the Night

Look into the night

Now tell me what you can see

Can you see yourself?

By Dakota Stanley

Looking Inside

I must look inside

Inside of myself to see

See what I can find

By Dakota Stanley

Trapped

O! What have I done?

I've forfeited my freedom

Forfeited for naught

By Dakota Stanley

My Heart

Much like a dead leaf

Falling from a dead tree branch

My heart has fallen

By Dakota Stanley

Question

I love you so much

Enough to face death for you

Would you do the same?

By Dakota Stanley

Reality

Money is neutral

It destroys all of our lives

Yet it brings hope

By Dakota Stanley

Crossing Over

Can you see me?

Can you hear me?

I'm scared to hear the response

In fact, I fear more the lack of one

It can't be! I am solid

A physical being

How can I go through walls?

I can't have passed on

I can't be dead

NO! NO! NO! NO!

Damn you! Damn myself! You must wake up

Yes! That's it. You're sleeping

You're dreaming vivid dreams

Don't cry mother, I'm only dreaming

If only I could wake myself, but how?

I'll go over and shake myself

Why won't I awake?

Could it really be?

Could I really be dead?

Mother!?! Can you see me?

Can you hear me?

By Dakota Stanley

Serpent's Kiss

Hello there, my fair lady

I shall greet you with a Serpent's Kiss

A bite upon the wrist

A kiss from a beast

A tender bite that represents my carnality

My carnality as well as my respect for you

A perfect harmony between beauty and beast

We together find balance

Consider my Serpent's Kiss an offering of myself

Through this kiss I offer my acquaintance

I assure you that this is truly an honor

For as a predator by nature, this is rare

Only those in a class of none other shall receive it

Be it is not a social class but one of which was earned through wisdom

On my knee I shall greet you

Greet you with a Serpent's Kiss

A symbol of my respect

My offering

For you, my fair lady

I shall greet with a Serpent's Kiss

By Dakota Stanley

Kissing the Cosmos

Open yourself to the cosmos

And they shall open to you

They shall welcome you with open arms

An open heart you must have

For truth of self, of what is, is necessary

They shall not judge for only you

It is only you who can judge yourself

Imperative is your ability to see

See not with your eyes, but with your heart

Your heart and soul's eyes open

To do this is truly divine, superb

You shall receive greatness, wisdom, and peace

As you kiss the cosmos, you kiss the limitless

You are only a slave to your rationality

Though 'tis only by choice

For if you open yourself to the cosmos

They shall open to you

By Dakota Stanley

Tree Of Life

Upon this Tree Of Life lie many fruits

Fruits in which we overlook

O! But these fruits are utterly delicious!

For they are grown with knowledge and love

Or is it the knowledge **OF** love

Maybe 'tis the love of knowledge

We must take a bite and see for ourselves

For upon the Tree Of Life lie many fruits

By Dakota Stanley

Freedom to Love

My heart aches for freedom

Freedom to find love again, unbroken

How will I be able to find inner peace?

Whoa, I am but a troubled soul

A troubled soul that seeks repair

Can what she's done be repaired?

Can you fix me?

Fix my heart?

My soul?

I cannot move on

Can't move on from the pain inside

I am but a slave to my own pain

My torture

My heart aches for freedom

Will you rescue me?

By Dakota Stanley

A Fire Inside

There is a fire inside of me

It burns, oh but it burns

It burns with rage, with hatred

The anger of the world's rejection

They rejected me

Should I reject them?

I should, but the question is, can I?

Can I turn away what I love?

Why must I love what only seeks to destroy?

For I've made mistakes

Mistakes in which only time can fix

Mistakes that have caused my peers to reject me

I shall love you!

I must redeem myself! I must!

For it is me who has failed you

O! Thank you world, I see now, eyes open

My eyes are open to what I have done

With renewed vigor I shall appease you

For there is a fire inside of me

One in which now burns with purpose

It burns to fuel my love for you

By Dakota Stanley

Section III: Resurrection

Twin Flames

She is my only love

Fallen from the skies above

She's been there through it all

When push has come to shove

She is my earthbound lover

There could never be another

These twin flames now light the sky

No longer undercover

She is the one for me who's best

She puts all others to the test

You make me smile, you make me laugh

You make my heart beat out my chest

Oh darling, darling, valentine

Your touch sends chills straight up my spine

I do not fear what I can feel

My love is yours for all of time.

By Dakota Stanley

<u>No Fear</u>

No, do not back down

Your fear will eat you alive

Fear none and prosper

A Lesson in Love

Life is the teacher

She teaches you how to love

Love is the lesson

By Dakota Stanley

Kheper

What is kheper?

Kheper is transformation

That of which we seek

By Dakota Stanley

Lilian

You are my daughter

My very reason to live

I love you, baby

By Dakota Stanley

See Yourself

You are beautiful

Can't you see your radiance?

Look at a mirror

By Dakota Stanley

<u>Epiphany of a Dark Saint</u>

At a very young age

My mother, she told me an important truth

She said, "Son, knowledge is power.

You must share your knowledge,

That of which is latent and learned."

I have come to recognize this as my duty

My duty to myself, to my society, and to the Creator

For this is my chosen path

Ultimately, my fate

I am but a dark saint with a purpose

A purpose that is light in nature

Bringing me 'round full circle

Perfect harmony

Perfect balance

Infinitely and eternally united

Unity found between light and dark

My life is dedicated to transformation

For with great power comes great responsibility

Knowledge, the greatest power of all

Followed by the greatest responsibility

To be patient, to teach, and to continue to learn

To grow

To transform

Because knowledge is power

By Dakota Stanley

<u>Magick</u>

There is magick all around us

Around us and inside us

From humans, to gods, and everything in between

There is magick

This is not the magick of parlor tricks

It is but the exertion of will

Whether be it the will of one or it be the will of many

Magick is a product of will

It is like any muscle

You must use it

When you use it, it shall grow stronger

You gain will-power

Everyone and everything can use magick

Plants, animals, people, all

Magick is there for us

Eternal

Immortal

It exists throughout the eons

There has always, and will always, be magick

Look deeply inside yourself

Feel your connection to everything

For there is magick all around us

By Dakota Stanley

<u>Beauty</u>

Let us take a moment to ponder the idea of beauty. Beauty is a concept that lies completely in the perception of that person who decides to use such a versatile word. But, does humanity tend to see beauty in the same light? For the most part; no. For instance, a mother, might find beauty by watching her child blossom into being, and the process of growth that is influenced directly by the nurturing that comes from the mother, whereas beauty in the eyes of the child could be all the unconditional love and support from his mother that has led to said child becoming the wonderful person they are today.

A fireman might see beauty in the miracle created by him where he saved someone from a fire, and in doing so, saved an entire family from the utter sense of hopelessness and oblivion that one feels by losing someone so dear to them. To the person he saved, they would see beauty in the act committed by the fireman wherein he risked his life and his loved ones' happiness and well-being for them (a complete stranger) so that they can exist.

An artist sees beauty in his ability to express himself through a painting, drawing, or poem so that some unknown faraway person can come closer to understanding themselves and their plight in life. Many viewers of aforementioned artistic talent note the beauty in the sway that this art has over them and how it effects the change and transformation that happens through their experience.

These are only a few examples of the plethora of beauty that can be seen, or better yet, perceived all around us meant only to open your eyes to the rest of the beauty life has to offer.

Now sit back, relax, and maybe even kick off your shoes. Close your eyes and reflect on what it is that you have just read, just experienced. As you read this, you begin to realize where it is that you find beauty. Your heart begins to swell and you begin to feel peace and bliss. As these emotions and feelings wash over you, an unadulterated smile spreads across your face. To me, **THAT** is beautiful.

By Dakota Stanley

Unique

Remember when in doubt of yourself

Remember there is no limit to what you can do

You are who you are

You've made yourself that way

You are forever changing, transforming

Caterpillar, you will be a butterfly

As you spread your wings the world shall see

We shall see all your beauty and splendor

Soaring ever higher, ever faster

You must be proud that you are different

Different, unique, this is your beauty, your strength

You are you, you are special, and remember

Remember that's why you're beautiful

Should you see this, see this as I do, see it as we do

You can accomplish anything you want

For there is no limit to what you can do

By Dakota Stanley

What Is Love

Love is quite strange, is it not?

We fight for love

We cry for love

At times, we even die for love

We spend our whole lives looking, searching

Trying to find love

Without it we are incomplete

Fragmented and lost

We become isolated

All for love

Is love a strength?

Could it be an affliction?

The answer lies with who it is you ask

We are beings of perception

Beings who love blindly, unconditionally

Why is this?

This concept lay mere inches from my grasp

O but love is quite strange, is it not?

By Dakota Stanley

<u>Land Of Many</u>

This is a land of many

Diversity is what makes us strong

Diverse are we, but in ways

But in ways we are similar

We love

We hate

We fight

We make peace

But in and at the end of the day

Though we are a land of many

We are but one

By Dakota Stanley

Made in the USA
Middletown, DE
25 September 2020